Neil and Sophie
Larden

Fingers Feet and Fun!

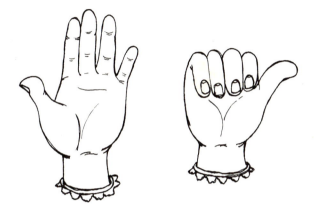

Fingers Feet and Fun!

New and traditional action rhymes and stories

Written and compiled by
DELPHINE EVANS
Illustrated by Sheila Carter

Hutchinson
London Melbourne Sydney Auckland Johannesburg

Hutchinson Children's Books Ltd
An imprint of the Hutchinson Publishing Group
17–21 Conway Street, London W1P 6JD

Hutchinson Publishing Group (Australia) Pty Ltd
PO Box 496, 16–22 Church Street, Hawthorne, Melbourne, Victoria 3122

Hutchinson Group (NZ) Ltd
32–34 View Road, PO Box 40-086, Glenfield, Auckland 10

Hutchinson Group (SA) Pty Ltd
PO Box 337, Bergvlei 2012, South Africa

First published 1984
Reprinted 1985

© Delphine Evans 1984
Illustrations © Sheila Carter 1984

Set in Plantin by
BookEns, Saffron Walden, Essex

Printed and bound in Great Britain by
Anchor Brendon Ltd, Tiptree, Essex

British Library Cataloguing in Publication Data
Evans, Delphine
    Fingers, feet and fun!
    I. Title
    784.6'2406   M1993

ISBN 0 09 156040 3

Contents

Introduction 11

1 **Walking Fingers** 13
Finger Rhymes

Walking Fingers 14
My Monkey 15
My Little House 15
Incy Wincy Spider 16
Mouse and Cat 16
Caterpillar 17
Two Little Dicky-birds 18
Sewing 19
Up the Tall White Candlestick 20
Round and Round the Garden 20
What Do You Suppose? 21
Arabella Miller 21
Hickory, Dickory, Dock 22

2 **Five Little Indians** 23
Counting Finger Rhymes

Five Little Fingers 24
One and One 25
Red Balloons 26
Five Little Indians 27
Five Fish Fingers 28
One, Two, Buckle My Shoe 29
Five Little Frogs 30
One, Two, Three, Four, Five 30

3 Can You Walk on Tiptoe? 31
Feet Rhymes

Hopping 32
Marching 32
Can You Walk on Tiptoe? 33
Jumping 33
Jump This Way 34
Running 35
This Little Piggy 36

4 Let's Pretend 37
Action Rhymes and Songs

Fingers, Toes, Head and Nose 38
Robin 38
Tiptoe 39
Tortoise 39
Peter Hammers 40
I'm a Little Teapot 41
The Washing Machine 41
There Was a Little Girl 42
Ring the Bell 42
Clocks 43
Little Robin Redbreast 44
Riding 45
Growing 46
What's Inside? 47
Miss Polly 48
Trees 49
Sleepy Baby 50
Old John Muddlecombe 50
Let's Pretend 51

Heads and Shoulders 52
Laughing Clowns 53
Work and Play 54
Polly Put the Kettle On 55
Mr Conductor 56
The Wheels on the Bus 58
Michael Finnigin 59
London Bridge 60
Baa-baa Black Sheep 61
Here We Go Round the Mulberry Bush 62
Ring a Ring of Roses 64

5 Sounds Fun! 65
Noise Stories and Rhymes

Farm 66
Weather 67
Seaside 68
Loud and Quiet 69
Farm Animals 70
Pat-a-Cake, Pat-a-Cake 70
Can You Whistle? 71
I Hear Thunder 72

6 Meet the Finger Family 73
Stories and Rhymes

Counting 74
Dressing Up 76
Scissors 78
Hello 79
Seeds 80
Up and Down 80

7 Just for Fun! 81

I Went Up the Stairs 82
My Mirror 82
Hide and Seek 83
Guinea Pig 83
Kinkajou, 84
Mr Nobody 84
Me 85
Losing Things 86
Keys 86
Mouse 86
Jack in the Box 87
Sometimes 87
My Son John 87
The Crooked Man 88
Piggy on the Railway 88
Dr Foster 88
Rain 89
Pictures 90
Splish, Splosh 89
The Little Nut Tree 90
The North Wind 90
Three Little Kittens 91
Three Little Rats 92
Pussy Cat, Pussy Cat 93
It's Raining 93
Safety Rhymes 94
Fireworks 94
In the Car 95
Colours 95
Look 96

8 Fingers, Feet and Fun! 97
All Kinds of Rhymes for Special Occasions

Making a Cake 98
Twinkle, Twinkle 99
Birthday Candles 100
I Am a Christmas Tree 101
Christmas is Coming 102
Crackers 102
My Card 103
Hot Cross Buns 103

Index of First Lines 105

INTRODUCTION

Rhymes are fun and learning through them is fun. Using mime to illustrate rhymes and songs encourages children to use their imagination and helps them to express themselves more easily in everyday life. This is very important in today's world when children are increasingly turning to television for entertainment and many creative forms of play are being lost.

Teaching and performing rhymes with young children is great fun and tremendously rewarding. Whether you are a teacher with a class full of lively children, or a parent or grandparent using the rhymes at home, you will find the children eager to learn and enthusiastic, especially when they themselves are asked to contribute to the rhymes by improvising.

While visiting schools and libraries to work with small children, I have found there is always a demand for new rhymes; especially for rhymes to suit particular occasions or situations; rhymes to perform sitting down or moving around for energetic play on the days when everyone wants to let off steam; and for celebrations like Christmas or birthdays. So along with the traditional favourites I have included lots of new rhymes in the collection, all of which have been tried and tested and proved popular. For easy reference you will find the rhymes divided into appropriate sections: finger rhymes, counting finger rhymes, noise rhymes, action rhymes and song rhymes for special occasions, and, of course, rhymes just for fun.

I have also included a few short stories in the collection; stories in which children can take an active part. In section 6 you can meet the Finger Family, always an immediate favourite. The fact that your fingers change into people, complete with faces and characters of their own, seems to hold a special magic for children. Then there are the noise stories – these often have children in fits of laughter as they try to guess the different sounds.

Children learn a great deal through performing rhymes; even the most simple finger play demands that children think about coordination. With action rhymes and songs, many more skills can be learnt – like jumping, hopping and skipping – not as easy for a small child as we might think. Learning to count, learning to recognize colours, and learning about life around us all come within the scope of a simple rhyme.

For parties, too, rhymes can be a great help. Often parties for small children present problems – particularly in games where there has to be a loser. All you need to do is turn to the section on special occasions to find entertaining rhymes that will keep children amused for hours. Try the noise rhymes to get rid of too much party excitement. The stories in this section are also great party favourites – especially if you record them. You can then sit back with the children afterwards for a good giggle.

Finally, I hope that parents, teachers and children will have as much fun using the rhymes as I have had in writing and selecting them. Do try to improvise – you will be surprised at how easy this is, and may even be inspired to write your own. After all, what more can you want than to find a reason for having fun?

Delphine Evans

1
Walking Fingers

Finger Rhymes

Walking Fingers

A family of fingers going for a walk.
    Right-hand fingers walking on left hand.
A family of fingers stopping for a talk.
    Fingers still.
'Hallo,' said the Mother. 'Hallo,' said the son.
    Wriggle first, then second finger.
'Hallo,' said the others. 'Hallo,' said everyone.
    Wriggle all fingers.
They walked to the top of a very steep hill.
    Walk fingers up left arm.
Everyone felt tired, so they sat quite still.
    Curl fingers up on shoulder.
They played a little game and scampered round and round.
    Wriggle fingers round on shoulder.
Then they all walked together – back to the ground.
    Walk fingers back down arm.
D. E.

My Monkey

My finger is a monkey
 Wriggle first finger.
Living in a zoo.
My finger is a monkey
 Point towards someone.
Looking straight at you!
The monkey climbs into a tree;
 Raise finger above head.
Now he's looking down at me!
 Look up at finger and point it down.

D. E.

My Little House

My little house won't stand up straight.
 Touch fingertips of both hands to form roof and rock hands from side to side.
My little house has lost its gate.
 Drop two little fingers.
My little house bends up and down.
 Sway hands.
My little house is the oldest one in town.
 Continue swaying hands.
Here comes the wind – it blows and blows again.
 Blow at hands.
Down falls my little house,
 Hands fall down.
Oh! What a shame!

Incy Wincy Spider

Incy Wincy Spider climbed up the spout.
Use fingers of both hands to make a spider climbing.
Down came the rain and washed poor Incy out.
Bring hands slowly down, like rain.
Out came the sunshine, dried up all the rain.
Spread hands and arms to indicate sunshine.
And Incy Wincy Spider climbed back up again.
As first line.

Mouse and Cat

One little mouse crept out one day,
One hand, two fingers creeping.
Eating the crumbs he found on the way.
Fingers stopping and 'nibbling'.
There sat a cat,
Other hand clenched.
Big and fat!
Move fist slightly.
One little mouse ran quickly back.
First hand moves away.
D. E.

Caterpillar

I can see a caterpillar
Wriggling on a leaf.
> *First finger one hand is caterpillar,*
> *other hand is leaf.*

It wriggles on the top and
It wriggles underneath.
> *Wriggle finger on palm,*
> *then underneath hand.*

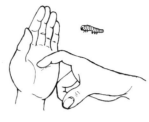

Then one day it's very still.
> *Rest finger on palm.*

I stand quietly watching till
It changes shape and falls asleep.
> *Half curl finger.*

Every day I take a peep.
Then at last, it moves about.
> *Wriggle finger.*

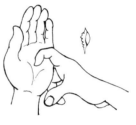

I'm so surprised, I give a shout.
For now there's a butterfly
Sitting on the leaf.
> *Hands spread out.*

It spreads its wings
And flies about.
> *Fly hands about.*

D. E.

Two Little Dicky-birds

Two little dicky-birds,
 Use index fingers and hold up.
Sitting on a wall.
One named Peter, one named Paul
 Wiggle each one in turn.

Fly away Peter, fly away Paul.
 Put appropriate fingers behind back.

Come back Peter,
 Bring back first finger.
Come back Paul.
 Bring back second finger.

Sewing

Come and watch me sewing – this is what I do:
I find a sewing basket and open it for you.
   Appropriate actions.
Next I look for cotton – find some coloured blue.
   Do sorting action and pull out cotton.
Wind some off the reel – now what do I do?
   Appropriate actions.

I remember – scissors next – snip, snip, snip and stop.
   Scissor action with fingers.
Now I thread the needle, push the cotton through the top.
   Mime.
Out it comes the other side, I can start to sew.
In and out and in and out and in and out I go!
   Sewing action.
D. E.

Up the Tall White Candlestick

Up the tall white candlestick
Hold left arm up for candlestick.
Crept little Mousie Brown;
Two fingers of right hand creep up arm.
Right to the top, but he couldn't get down.
Keep fingers at top of arm.
So he called to his Grandma,
'Grandma, Grandma!'
Call loudly.
But Grandma was in town.
So he curled himself into a ball –
Clench fingers into a fist.
And rolled himself down.
Roll fist down arm.

Round and Round the Garden

Round and round the garden,
Run your first finger round the child's palm.
Like a teddy bear.
One step,
Finger walks up child's arm.
Two steps,
Tickly under there.
Tickle under arm.

Arabella Miller

Little Arabella Miller
Found a hairy caterpillar.
> *Pretend to hold caterpillar.*

First it crawled upon her mother,
> *Make it crawl on someone.*

Then it crawled upon her brother.
> *Make it crawl on someone else.*

All said, 'Arabella Miller,
> *All together.*

Take away that caterpillar!'

What Do You Suppose?

What do you suppose?
A bee sat on my nose.
> *First finger on nose.*

Then what do you think?
He gave me a wink,
> *Wink one eye.*

And said, 'I beg your pardon,
I thought you were the garden.'
> *Make finger fly away.*

Hickory, Dickory, Dock

Hickory, dickory, dock
Clap three times.
The mouse ran up the clock.
Run two fingers up left arm.
The clock struck one,
Clap once.
And down he ran,
Run fingers down arm.
Hickory, dickory, dock.
Clap three times.

2
Five Little Indians

Counting Finger Rhymes

Five Little Fingers

Five little fingers walked across my lap.
> *Hold fingers straight up, then walk them across lap.*

One became tired and stopped for a nap.
> *Curl thumb up.*

Four little fingers walked across my knee.
> *Hold up four, then walk them across knee.*

One fell off and that left three.
> *Curl up another.*

Three little fingers dancing all around.
> *Hold up three and make them dance.*

One became lost – only two were found.
> *Curl up another.*

Two little fingers go up my arm for fun.
> *Hold up two, then walk them up arm.*

One couldn't make it – now there's only one.
> *Curl up another.*

One little finger, left all alone.
> *Hold it up and wriggle it.*

Cried and cried and cried until the others came home!
> *Flick all fingers up straight.*

D. E.

One and One

One finger and one finger –
> *One finger raised on each hand.*

That makes two.
Now we know just what to do.
> *Tap fingers together.*

Two fingers and two fingers –
> *Two fingers raised on each hand.*

That makes four.
Can we think of any more?
> *Tap fingers together.*

Three fingers and three fingers –
> *Actions as above.*

That makes six,
Standing up straight, just like sticks.

Four fingers and four fingers –
That makes eight.
What comes next? Just you wait.

Five fingers and five fingers –
That makes ten.
Clap our hands and start again.
> *Clap hands and repeat rhyme.*

D. E.

Red Balloons

Five red round balloons
    Hold hand up, fingers spread outwards.
High up in the sky.
    Move hand above head.
I tried to catch one
As they went floating by.
    Stretch arm, and pretend to grasp at balloons.
'STOP!' I called,
'Please, please, STOP!'
One came slowly down
    *Curl up four fingers and bring one
    down slowly.*
And
  then
    went
      POP!
    Say slowly and clap loudly!

Four red round balloons etc.
    *Hand back above head and continue until no
    balloons are left.*

No red round balloons
    Look upwards.
High up in the sky.
They
  have
    all
      gone
        POP!
    Extra big clap.
D. E.

Five Little Indians

Five little Indians dancing round and round,
   One hand with fingers dancing.
Making Indian noises, what a happy sound.
One little Indian tripped and hurt his nose.
   Bend one finger over.
Four little Indians dancing on their toes.
   Four dancing.
One little Indian resting on a seat.
   Another away.
Three little Indians dancing on their feet.
   Three dancing.
One little Indian turned away to sneeze.
   Another away.
Two little Indians kicking up their knees.
   Two dancing.
One little Indian tired himself out.
   Another away.
Then all the little Indians gave an Indian shout.
   Shout.
'Let's go back and dance again, round and round
   and round.'
   All pop up.
Five little Indians – what a happy sound.
D. E.

Five Fish Fingers

Five fish fingers – spread out on the plate.
> *Five fingers spread out.*

I like to eat them – they taste just great!

Five fish fingers – not one more.
Take a big bite – now there's four.
> *Pretend to eat thumb and then keep curled up.*

Four fish fingers – just for me.
Take a big bite – now there's three.
> *Curl up first finger.*

Three fish fingers – what shall I do?
Take a big bite – now there's two.
> *Pretend to eat second finger.*

Two fish fingers – oh, what fun.
Take a big bite – now there's one.
> *Pretend to eat third finger.*

One fish finger – left all alone.
Take a big bite – now there's none!
> *Pretend to eat fourth finger then clench fist.*

D. E.

One, Two, Buckle My Shoe

One, two, buckle my shoe.
> *Count one, two on fingers then pretend to buckle shoe.*

Three, four, knock on the door.
> *Count and do actions as before. Continue until you think you've reached the numbers the child can remember.*

Five, six, pick up sticks.
Seven, eight, lay them straight.
Nine, ten, a big fat hen.
Eleven, twelve, dig and delve.
Thirteen, fourteen, maids a courting.
Fifteen, sixteen, maids a kissing.
Seventeen, eighteen, maids awaiting.
Nineteen, twenty, my plate's empty!

Five Little Frogs

Five little frogs sitting on a well.
> *Hold up five fingers.*

One looked in and down he fell.
> *Bend one finger over.*

Frogs jump high.
> *Lift hand.*

Frogs jump low.
> *Lower hand.*

Four little frogs dancing to and fro.
> *Keep finger curled up and sway hand.*

Four little frogs sitting on a well *etc.*
Continue as above, reducing number of fingers held up for each verse.

One, Two, Three, Four, Five

One, two, three, four, five,
> *Count each finger.*

Once I caught a fish alive.
> *Pretend to catch fish.*

Six, seven, eight, nine, ten,
> *Count each finger on other hand.*

Then I let it go again.
> *Pretend to throw fish back.*

Why did you let him go?
Because he bit my finger so.
> *Shake right hand.*

Which finger did he bite?
The little finger on the right.
> *Hold up little finger on right hand.*

3
Can You Walk on Tiptoe?

Feet Rhymes

Hopping

Two feet together, then lift up one.
> *Appropriate actions.*

Jump with the other, what have I done?
I have made a hop!
I will never stop!
Hopping, hopping, hopping.
Never ever stopping.
> *Continue hopping until everyone is tired!*

D. E.

Marching

Arrange children in pairs in centre of room.
Marching, marching, marching two by two.
> *March along.*

Marching, marching, like soldiers do.
Marching, marching, arms to and fro.
Marching, marching, up and down we go.
Marching, marching, marching on our own.
> *Separately.*

Marching, marching, marching back to home!
> *Everyone back to centre.*

D. E.

Can You Walk on Tiptoe?

Can you walk on tiptoe,
As softly as a cat?
> *Walk softly on tiptoe.*

And can you stamp along the road,
Stamp, stamp, just like that?
> *Stamp around.*

Can you take some great big strides,
Like a giant can?
> *Great big strides.*

Or walk along so slowly,
Like a poor, bent old man?
> *Bend over and walk slowly.*

Jumping

Feet together, standing still.
> *Appropriate action.*

I can jump, I will, I will!
> *Get ready to jump.*

Feet together, here I go.
> *Start jumping.*

Jumping fast, jumping slow!
> *Appropriate actions.*

D. E.

Jump This Way

Jumping, jumping – jumping man,
Jump up and down on the same spot.
Jumping, jumping where I am.
Continue jumping.
Jump one forward – forwards now,
Jump one forward, then another one.
Jump one forward – take a bow.
Jump one more forward and bow.
Jump one backward – very slow,
Jump one backward, then one more.
Jump one backward – backwards go.
Jump backwards twice.
Jump to the side – that's hard to do,
Jump sideways twice.
Jump to the other – that's hard too!
Jump twice to the other side.
Now –
One forward – one backwards and sideways as well.
One jump each way.
I'm tired now – I can always tell.
Pretend to be tired.
Down to the floor, it's time for a sleep.
Curl up or sit.
Close my eyes tightly – not even a peep!
Close eyes and pretend to sleep.
D. E.

Running

Running, running, on the spot.
> *Run on the spot.*

Running, running, makes me hot.
> *Continue.*

Running, running, nowhere to go.
> *Continue.*

Where am I going?
  I don't know!
> *Shrug shoulders and stop.*

D. E.

This Little Piggy

Wiggle each toe in turn, starting with the big one.

This little piggy went to market,
This little piggy stayed home.
This little piggy had roast beef,
This little piggy had none.
This little piggy cried, 'Wee-wee-wee,
I can't find my way home.'

4
Let's Pretend

Action Rhymes and Songs

Fingers, Toes, Head and Nose

Do all the actions as the rhyme suggests.

Wriggle your fingers
    and wriggle your toes.
Nod your head
    and twitch your nose.
Now stand up
    and now sit down.
Roll your hands around
    and around.

Repeat from the beginning as many times as you like.

Everyone's tired
    so let's go to sleep.
Everyone's quiet
    not even a peep!
Eyes closed for a nice quiet moment.
D. E.

Robin

Little Robin Redbreast,
Sat upon a rail.
Niddle-naddle went his head,
    Waggle head.
Wiggle-waggle went his tail.
    Wiggle bottom.

Tiptoe

Do the actions as suggested.

Tiptoe softly like a mouse.
Tiptoe, tiptoe, all round the house.

Stretch your arms up like the trees.
Wave your branches in the breeze.

Be a hedgehog round and small,
Curled into a prickly ball.

Soldiers marching up and down.
Marching, marching, all round the town.
D. E.

Tortoise

A tortoise has a house that goes everywhere
   with it.
   Curl up on floor.
Not too big, not too small – a perfect fit.
He can stay inside, if there's rain about.
   Head tucked in.
And if the sun is shining, then he can come out.
   Pop head up.
In the winter when it's cold, he curls up small.
   Head in, curl up tightly.
He stays inside until it's warm –
   we don't see him at all.
D. E.

Peter Hammers

Peter hammers with one hammer.
One fist banging on lap.
One hammer, one hammer.
Peter hammers with one hammer,
All day long.

Peter hammers with two hammers,
Two fists banging.
Continue as first verse.

Peter hammers with three hammers,
Two fists and one foot banging.

Peter hammers with four hammers,
Two fists, two feet banging.

Peter hammers with five hammers,
Two fists, two feet banging, head nodding.

Peter's very tired now,
Rest hands on head.
Tired now, tired now.
Peter's very tired now
Go to sleep.
Close eyes for a few seconds.

Peter's wide awake now,
Lift head and stretch.
Awake now, awake now.
Peter's wide awake now.
Start again.
Repeat the rhyme at double speed.

I'm a Little Teapot

I'm a little teapot, short and stout;
  Make yourself stout.
Here's my handle, here's my spout.
  One hand on hip, other arm as a spout.
When I see the teacups, hear me shout,
'Tip me up and pour me out.'
  Tip slowly to the side of the spout.

The Washing Machine

Washing in the washing machine,
  going round and round.
    Rotate arms round each other.

Washing in the washing machine,
  moving up and down.
    Arms up and down.

Round and round and up and down,
  Round, then up and down.
It makes a noisy sound.

Faster, faster, faster,
  round and round and round.
    Rotate arms faster.

D. E.

There Was a Little Girl

There was a little girl,
Who had a little curl,
Right in the middle of her forehead.
Indicate.

When she was good,
She was very, very good,
Angelic expressions.

But when she was bad
Naughty expressions.
She was horrid.
All pull faces and then say boo!

Ring the Bell

Ring the bell,
Pull a lock of hair.
Knock at the door,
Tap forehead.
Lift up the latch,
Pull nose.
And walk in!
Open mouth and 'walk' finger in.

Clocks

The big old clock,
> *Stand tall.*

Goes tick-tock, tick-tock.
> *Loud voice, slow sway from side to side.*

That is the noise of the
Big old clock.
Dong, Dong, Dong.
> *Move back and forwards slowly.*

The middle-sized clock,
> *Stand normally.*

Goes tick-tock, tick-tock, tick-tock,
> *Normal voice, steady sway.*

That is the noise of the
Middle-sized clock.
Ding-dong, ding-dong, ding-dong.
> *Move back and forwards steadily.*

The little cuckoo clock,
Goes tick-tock, tick-tock, tick-tock.
> *Quiet voice, quick sway.*

That is the noise of the
Little cuckoo clock.
Cuckoo, cuckoo, cuckoo.
> *Move back and forwards quickly.*

D. E.

Little Robin Redbreast

Bring fingertips and thumb of right hand together for robin. Left hand clenched for cat.

Little Robin Redbreast sat upon a tree.
Raise right hand above head.
Up went Pussy Cat and down went he.
Raise left hand then lower right hand.
Down came Pussy and away Robin ran.
Lower left hand, move right hand to side.
Says little Robin Redbreast, 'Catch me if you can.'

Little Robin Redbreast jumped upon a wall.
Raise right hand.
Pussy Cat jumped after him and almost had a fall.
Raise left hand, lower right hand.
Little Robin chirped and sang and what did Pussy say?
Pussy Cat said, 'Mew', and Robin ran away.
Right hand to the side.

Riding

Sit on a chair.
Riding in a train I go,
Rocking, rocking to and fro.
  Rock to and fro.
Side to side and to and fro.
Riding in a train I go.

Stand.
In an aeroplane I fly,
Up, up, up, into the sky.
  Wave arms pretending to fly.
Up, up, up, so very high.
In an aeroplane I fly.

Lie on the floor.
Riding on my bike today,
Pedal, pedal, all the way.
  Legs in the air pedalling.
Pedal fast and pedal slow,
Riding on my bike I go.
D. E.

Growing

See me curl up very small
Curl up on floor.
Like a little tiny ball.
Moving upward very slow
Gradually move on to knees.
Up and up like people grow.

Now upon my knees I kneel,
Kneel.
I am growing, I can feel.
Start moving.
Moving upwards very slow,
Move slowly on to feet.
Up and up like people grow.

Now I'm standing straight and tall.
Stand straight and tall.
I think I'd rather be a ball.
Gradually start to go down again.
Slowly, slowly to the floor.
Right down into a ball.
Now I'll do it all once more!
D. E.

What's Inside?

Start off curled up on floor.

I'm inside an egg, with a shell all round,
Curled up quietly on the ground.
    Very still.
Still and quiet I stay.
Until one day –
I start to grow.
    Start to uncurl.
I tap my shell from down below.
    *Move on to knees and pretend
    to tap shell over head.*
No longer still
    Continue tapping all round.
Tap, tap, until –
I pop right out.
    Jump up.
It's like a trick,
Just look at me –
I'm a BABY CHICK!
    Shake and flap wings etc.
D. E.

Miss Polly

Miss Polly had a dolly,
Fold arms as if holding baby.
Who was sick, sick, sick,
So she phoned for the doctor,
Pretend to use telephone.
To come quick, quick, quick,
The doctor came,
with his bag and his hat,
and he knocked on the door,
Pretend to knock on door.
With a tat-atat-a-tat.
He looked at the dolly
and he shook his head.
Look at imaginary baby and shake head.
Then he said, 'Miss Polly,
Shake finger.
Put her straight to bed.'
He wrote on a paper,
Pretend to write.
For a pill, pill, pill,
'I'll be back in the morning,
Wave goodbye.
With my bill, bill, bill.'

Trees

If I could wish what I could be,
I would like to be a tree.
I might grow straight and very tall,
   Stand straight and tall.
And I'd look down upon you all.
   Look down.
I might have branches, bushy and wide,
   Spread arms outward.
Where all the birds would come and hide.
Tall or wide, whichever I was,
   Stretch arms up then out.
I know what would happen in the wind, because
All trees wave their branches about,
   Start waving arms.
When the wind blows in and out.
But when the sun shines and it's hot,
Underneath would be a shady spot.
   Look down.
Trees are useful, trees are fun.
I wish, I wish, that I was one!

D. E.

Sleepy Baby

I am a baby fast asleep.
> *Eyes closed, head resting on hands.*

I open my eyes to take a peep.
> *Open eyes.*

I lift up my head to look around.
> *Lift head and look around.*

I open my mouth – make a yawning sound.
> *Yawn.*

I lift up my arms and stretch up high.
> *Stretch.*

I think I might be going to cry.
> *Arms down, sad face.*

Oh no, I won't, I'll go back to sleep.
> *Head resting on hands again.*

I'll close my eyes and not even peep!
> *Close eyes and be very still.*

D. E.

Old John Muddlecombe

Old John Muddlecombe lost his cap,
> *Put hands on head.*

He couldn't find it anywhere, the poor old chap.
> *Pretend to look for hat.*

He walked down the high street,
> *Walk slowly round the room.*

And everybody said:
'Silly John Muddlecombe –
You've got it on your *head*!'
> *Shake finger and then put hands on head.*

Let's Pretend

Let's pretend to be a frog,
　Curl up on floor.
Hiding underneath a log.
I'm a frog, I'm a frog,
　Head popping up.
Hiding underneath a log.

Let's pretend to be a man,
Hammering, hammering, hard as I can.
　Standing or sitting hammering.
I'm a man, I'm a man,
Hammering, hammering, hard as I can.

Let's pretend to be a lady,
Rocking to sleep a tiny baby.
　*Sitting and rocking
　pretend baby in arms.*
I'm a lady, I'm a lady,
Rocking to sleep a tiny baby.

Let's pretend to be a robin,
Hopping, hopping, bobbin', bobbin'.
　Jumping about and hopping.
I'm a robin, I'm a robin,
Hopping, hopping, bobbin', bobbin'.
D. E.

Heads and Shoulders

To the tune of 'There is a Tavern in the Town'.

Heads and shoulders, knees and toes, knees and toes;
Touch each in turn.
Heads and shoulders, knees and toes, knees and toes.
Eyes and ears and mouth and nose;
Point to each in turn.
Heads and shoulders, knees and toes, knees and toes!

Laughing Clowns
To the tune of 'Pop Goes the Weasel'.

Lots and lots of funny clowns,
See the way we wobble.
Wobble.
Side to side and to and fro;
Appropriate actions.
Over we topple!

We are silly wobbly clowns,
Wobble faster.
Laughing as we wobble.
Side to side and to and fro;
Over we topple!
D. E.

Work and Play
To the Tune of 'Here We Go Round the Mulberry Bush'.

When we wake up, we jump out of bed,
 Stretch and jump.
Jump out of bed, jump out of bed.
When we wake up, we jump out of bed,
Sometimes we work, sometimes we play.

We put on our clothes and our socks and shoes,
 Mime.
Socks and shoes, socks and shoes.
We put on our clothes and our socks and shoes,
Sometimes we work, sometimes we play.

D. E.

Polly Put the Kettle On

Polly put the kettle on,
Polly put the kettle on,
   Pretend to put kettle on.
Polly put the kettle on;
We'll all have tea.

Sukey take it off again,
   Pretend to take kettle off.
Sukey take it off again,
Sukey take it off again,
They're all gone away.

Mr Conductor
To the tune of 'Old Macdonald'.

This song can be done in many ways, according to the age of the children:
1. *Using pretend instruments with the children making the noises and actions.*
2. *As above, but giving groups of children different instruments. On the last verse they all play together.*
3. *As 2, but using real instruments.*

Mis-ter Con-duc-tor had a band, Rum-tidd-ly um-tum-

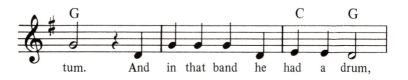
tum. And in that band he had a drum,

rum-tidd-ly-um-tum-tum. With a boom-boom here, and a

boom-boom there, Here a boom, there a boom,

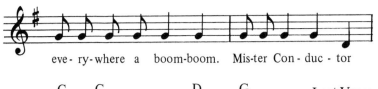

Mr Conductor had a band,
Rum, tiddly, um, tum, tum.
And in that band he had a drum,
Rum, tiddly, um, tum, tum.
With a boom-boom here and a boom-boom there,
Here a boom, there a boom, everywhere a boom-boom.
Mr Conductor had a band,
Rum, tiddly, um, tum, tum.

Repeat verse substituting the following instruments:
Piano: tinkle-tinkle.
Cymbal: clash-clash.
Trumpet: tra-la, tra-la.
Bell: ding-dong.
Whistle: oo-oo, oo-oo.

Encourage children to think of other instruments.
D. E.

The Wheels on the Bus
To the tune of 'Merrily We Roll Along'

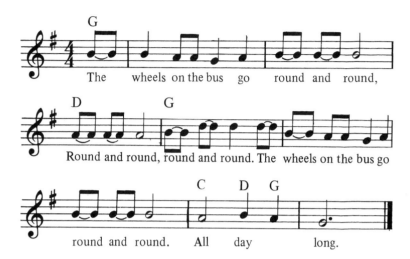

The wheels on the bus go round and round,
Rotate arms round each other.
Round and round, round and round.
Continue rotating arms.
The wheels on the bus go round and round.
All day long.

The bell on the bus goes ding-a-ling-a-ling,
Pretend to ring bell.
Ding-a-ling-a-ling, ding-a-ling-a-ling,
The bell on the bus goes ding-a-ling-a-ling,
All day long.

This song is ideal for improvising. Children have great fun thinking up their own actions and sounds.

Michael Finnigin

There was an old man called Michael Finnigin.
He grew whiskers on his chinnigin.
The wind came up and blew them in again.
Poor old Michael Finnigin begin again.

London Bridge

London Bridge is falling down,
    Use arms to make bridge.
Falling down, falling down.
    Hands fall to lap.
London Bridge is falling down,
My fair lady.

Build it up with iron bars,
    Pretend to build.
Iron bars, iron bars,
Build it up with iron bars,
My fair lady.

Iron bars will bend and bow,
    Bend hands.
Bend and bow etc.

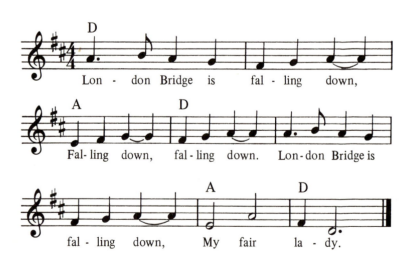

Baa-baa Black Sheep

Baa-baa black sheep,
Have you any wool?
Yes sir, yes sir,
Three bags full.
   Hold up three fingers.
One for the master,
   Count first finger.
One for the dame,
   Count second finger.
And one for the little boy
   Count the last finger.
Who lives down the lane.

Here We Go Round the Mulberry Bush

During the first verse, children hold hands and skip round in a circle.

Here we go round the mul-berry bush, The mul-berry bush, the mul-berry bush. Here we go round the mul-berry bush, On a cold and Fros-ty mor-ning.

Here we go round the mulberry bush,
The mulberry bush, the mulberry bush.
Here we go round the mulberry bush,
On a cold and frosty morning.

This is the way we sweep the floor,
> *Mime.*

Sweep the floor, sweep the floor, *etc.*

This is the way we wash our clothes, *etc.*
> *Mime.*

Continue the song encouraging the children to think up their own actions. When everyone's had enough, end the song with:

This is the way we go to bed,
> *Mime.*

Go to bed, go to bed,
This is the way we go to bed,
On a cold and frosty evening.

Ring a Ring of Roses

Ring a ring of roses,
All stand in a circle.
A pocket full of posies,
Skip around, holding hands.
A-tishoo, a-tishoo,
We all fall down.
All fall down.

The king has sent his daughter,
To fetch a pail of water,
A-tishoo, a-tishoo,
We all fall down.

The robin on the steeple,
Is singing to the people,
A-tishoo, a-tishoo,
We all fall down.

5
Sounds Fun!

Noise Stories and Rhymes

With the stories, go through the different noises with the children before you begin, getting them to guess each one. Start the stories when you feel they have mastered all the sounds.

Farm

Make the appropriate noises wherever dashes appear.

Mr Clapp — was a farmer who loved horses —. Although he had to keep cows — and sheep — and pigs — and chickens — his favourite animal was still the horse —.

He wouldn't have a tractor — on his farm. He used his horse — to do all the things a tractor — usually does.

When he ploughed his fields, he walked behind his horse — with his dog — and because there was no tractor noise — he could hear the birds singing — especially the cuckoo —. Sometimes he even heard a tiny field mouse —.

Once a month he got up early to milk his cows — feed the pigs — and chickens — and groom his horse — ready to take him to market.

As soon as he had finished eating his breakfast — and drinking his tea — he trotted down the road — on his horse — whistling — as he rode along. Mr Clapp — was a happy farmer!

D. E.

Weather

Make the appropriate noises wherever dashes appear.

Susan wants to lie in bed and listen to the wind — and the rain — but she has to get up.

In the bathroom she turns on the taps — to wash. Then she goes downstairs — and starts her breakfast. She has crackling cereal — and a drink —. Now she is ready to go shopping with her mother.

Still the wind is blowing — and she splashes — through the puddles; her wellies are a bit too big and make a flip-flop noise —.

On the way, Susan can hear thunder in the distance —. Her mother decides to hurry — and Susan's wellies flip-flop faster — making big splashes in the puddles —. Still the wind is blowing —.

Inside the supermarket, music is playing — and when they pay for the shopping the till goes —.

When they go outside again the wind is still blowing — and the thunder is getting louder —and it's starting to rain — so they ride home on a bus —.

Susan and her mother are pleased to be home again, but still the wind is blowing — and the rain is raining — and the thunder is thundering — and now there are lightning flashes — but Susan doesn't mind, in fact she quite likes all the weather noises!

D. E.

Seaside

Make the appropriate noises wherever dashes appear.

Mary and Mark are going to the seaside. They love to watch the waves splashing — sometimes hard and loud — and sometimes soft and gentle —.

On the day of their visit they get up very early, as soon as the alarm clock goes —. They say goodbye to their cat — and jump into the back of the car —. The car doesn't want to start — but eventually they are on their way —.

At last they can see the sea and the waves — they can even hear the seagulls screaming — waiting for someone to feed them.

They make sandcastles and paddle — and they even have a ride on a donkey —. A long way out in the sea they notice a motor boat — going faster and faster —. All the children on the beach are making happy noises — but soon it's time to go home.

On the way back it starts to rain —. The windscreen wipers are going — and other cars are hooting — but at last they arrive home, very tired and yawning —.

Soon they are both in bed and fast asleep — dreaming of the waves splashing in and out —.

D. E.

Loud and Quiet

Quietly, quietly, not a sound.
> *Whisper with fingers on lips.*

I'm listening and listening,
As I look around.
> *Look around.*

No sound as I nod,
No sound as I clap,
> *Hands together softly in clapping action.*

No sound as I tap my hands upon my lap.

LOUDLY, LOUDLY, STAMP AND CLAP!
> *Say loudly and stamp and clap.*

Stamp and clap, stamp and clap.

LOUDLY, LOUDLY, STAMP AND CLAP!
> *As loud as possible.*

All that noise –
        well
                fancy that!

D. E.

Farm Animals

A cow goes moo – its calf goes maa.
A dog goes woof – a sheep goes baa-aa.

A pig goes grunt – a chicken goes cluck.
Neigh goes a horse – quack goes a duck!

A cat goes miaow – its kitten goes mew.
And a cockerel crows cock-a-doodle-doo!
D. E.

Pat-a-Cake, Pat-a-Cake

This is a hand-clapping rhyme.

Pat-a-cake, pat-a-cake,
Baker's man.
Bake me a cake
As fast as you can.
Pat it and prick it
And mark it with B.
Put it in the oven,
For baby and me.

Can You Whistle?

Do the appropriate actions.

Push your lips out –
   keep them together tight.
Leave a little hole –
   get it just right.
Move your tongue –
   give a gentle blow.
If you can whistle –
   you will soon know!
D. E.

I Hear Thunder

I hear thunder, I hear thunder,
> *Stamp feet on the floor.*

Hark, don't you, hark, don't you?
> *Pretend to listen.*

Pitter-patter raindrops,
> *Indicate rain with fingers.*

Pitter-patter raindrops.
I'm wet through –
> *Shake body.*

SO ARE YOU!
> *Point to a neighbour.*

6
Meet the Finger Family

Stories and Rhymes

Notes for use with all Finger Family stories.

You will get the best effect from Finger Family stories if you read them through first. A list of props is given at the beginning of each one. If you do not have the exact things, it should be quite easy to find substitutes.

Always start the stories by drawing the faces on your fingers and introducing each one to the children as you do so:

This is Tommy Thumb, who looks after the Finger Family.

This is Freddie First Finger, who is always poking himself into trouble.

Susie Second Finger does her best to stop him.

Next is Timothy Third Finger, who is almost as big as Freddie, but better behaved.

Last of all there's Lucy Little Finger, who is always good because she is so tiny.

Counting

*Props: Use a black felt-tip pen to mark the faces.
After you have introduced the characters to the children, curl up your fingers.*

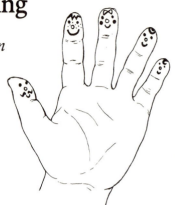

The Finger Family are trying to learn a counting rhyme. Tommy Thumb has to start and he pops up, standing straight and tall, saying:
'Everyone knows I'm Tommy Thumb,
I'll start off – I'm number one.'
  Next Freddie stood up, but he could never remember his number, so Tommy continued:
'Freddie never knows what to do,
But we all know he's number two.'
  Then it was Susie and as she uncurled, she said:
'I am Susie, you can see.
I know my number – it is three'.
  Timothy was next and he found it difficult to remember too. Susie gave him a nudge and said: 'Come on Timothy, try once more,' and he popped up and replied, 'Oh, yes, I know – I'm number four.'
  Now only Little Lucy was left curled up. Together they all said:
'Little Lucy is trying to hide,

We all know she's number five.'

Lucy popped up and stood beside them – a very tiny number five.

'Let's see if we can remember the numbers without the rhyme,' said Tommy Thumb. 'Everyone curl up and I'll do the counting.

'One, two, three, four, five.'

When they looked around, only four fingers were standing up – Freddie had fallen asleep!

'Let's wake him,' said Susie and they all shouted: 'FREDDIE FIRST FINGER!'

He jumped up quickly – so that once more there were five fingers standing straight and tall.

'Right,' said Tommy Thumb. 'Once more with the rhyme,' and they curled up again.

Hold up appropriate fingers.

'Everyone knows – I'm Tommy Thumb,
I'll start off – I'm number one.
Freddie never knows what to do,
But we all know – he's number two.'

'I am Susie – you can see,
I know my number – it is three.
Come on Timothy try once more.'

'Oh, yes, I know – I'm number four.'

'Little Lucy, trying to hide,
We all know – she's number five!'

Because they all got it right,
They all curled up and said goodnight.
D. E.

Dressing Up

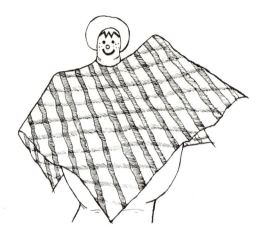

Props: Black felt-tip pen. Junk box containing in particular ribbon, wool, a sticky paper circle, a piece of material (the size of a small hanky) with a hole in the centre.

The Finger Family had decided to play a dressing-up game. Tommy Thumb and Susie Second Finger were taking things out of a box of junk. Freddie First Finger was just watching. Timothy Third Finger and Little Lucy were deciding what they would like to be.

There were pieces of ribbon and material, old containers, bits of wool and paper and buttons. Susie found a long piece of ribbon.

'Help me hold it, please Tommy,' she said and they started to pull it out of the box.

Little Lucy was laughing because it was so long.

When it was right out of the box, they wriggled it around and it looked like a snake.

Even Freddie was laughing at the pretend snake. He wriggled himself and pretended he was a snake too.

'Let's see what else is in there,' he said and they all followed Freddie inside.

Tommy held up something he had found. 'Look at this,' he said. 'It's some material with a hole in the middle.'

Susie Second Finger helped Tommy hold it up for everyone to see and Freddie pushed himself through the hole.

Tommy and Susie were wriggling underneath and they looked like a hand puppet. Freddie was the head and Tommy was one arm, with Susie, Timothy and Lucy the other.

Freddie bent over and told them to clap. 'We are clever,' he said. 'Now Tommy if you wriggle, it will look as if you are waving.'

Freddie decided he needed a hat, so he jumped into the box again. He found a sticky paper circle which just fitted on the top of his head and as he jumped out he shouted, 'This is fun.'

There were quite a lot of things they found they could do when they were a pretend puppet and they played for a long time. But their favourite game of all was singing, 'We all clap hands together.'

It's very easy to make your hand into a puppet like the Finger Family did. Try it and see!

D. E.

Scissors

Props: Sewing box, with various things inside, including a length of thread and pointed scissors. Felt-tip pen. Plaster.

Freddie had found the sewing basket and was poking about inside. Susie Second Finger and Tommy Thumb were doing their best to get him out.

'Freddie, will you please come out,' said Susie.

Now it was Tommy Thumb's turn. 'Freddie, if you don't come out on your own, Susie and I will pull you out.'

'All right, Tommy,' Freddie replied. 'I'll come out if you help me hold this snake.'

Little Lucy and Timothy curled up tight – they didn't like snakes.

'It's not a real one,' Freddie told them. 'It's a piece of thread – it just looks like a snake.'

Tommy helped him hold it and together they wriggled it around.

Little Lucy thought it was fun and laughed a lot – until it became muddled up and knotted.

'Now look what you've done,' said Freddie. 'It's tied itself up – now I'll have to cut it. Come on Tommy, back into the sewing box, I saw some scissors in there.'

'Those were sharp pointed ones,' said Susie. 'We don't use those, we only use the ones with round ends.'

'I don't care,' said Freddie, and he jumped back into the box, taking the rest of the Finger Family with him.

There was a yell and Freddie came back out, looking very hurt. He had jumped in right on top of the pointed-end scissors. It was a good job the others had curled themselves up, because Freddie had to have a plaster put on him and only the tip of him could be seen.

He made a terrible fuss, but no one felt sorry for him.

'Serves you right,' said Tommy Thumb. 'You should listen to what I tell you.' Freddie kept very quiet for the rest of the day.

D. E.

Introduce the rhymes in the same way as the stories, by painting faces on your fingers.

Hello

The Finger Family thinks it's night.
Finger Family curled up tight.
   Fingers curled up.
Finger Family fast asleep;
Finger Family do not peep.

Finger Family wake up now.
   Uncurl and stretch fingers.
Finger Family take a bow.
   Bend fingers, then ask the children to say hello to each character in turn.

D. E.

Seeds

The Finger Family want to play
    Hold fingers up.
A pretending game with you today.
They are seeds inside a pot;
    Curl fingers up.
I wonder will they grow or not?
Freddie's moving – what will he be?
    Uncurl forefinger.
He's growing tall – just like a tree.
    Stretch forefinger.
Tommy's next and Susie too,
    Uncurl next two fingers.
Then Timothy and Lucy, what will they do?
    Stretch all fingers.
All the family have grown into trees,
Swaying gently in the breeze.
    Sway fingers from side to side.

D. E.

Up and Down

Up, up, up and up so high;
    Stretch arm upwards.
Finger Family in the sky.
Down again, they slowly come.
    Lower arm slowly.
Have a rest now that is done.
    Curl fingers up.

D. E.

7
Just for Fun!

I Went Up the Stairs

Adult: I went up one pair of stairs.
Child: Just like me.
Adult: I went up two pairs of stairs.
Child: Just like me.
Adult: I went into a room.
Child: Just like me.
Adult: I looked out of the window.
Child: Just like me.
Adult: And there I saw a monkey.
Child: Just like me!

Now change roles.

My Mirror

I looked in the mirror
And who did I see?
Someone else looking – just like me!

There was a mouth,
There was a nose.
Right at the bottom – I could see toes!

I waved my hand,
Someone waved too.
'Mummy, mummy – what shall I do?'

Mummy came quickly,
And what did I see?
There were two someones – Mummy and me!
D. E.

Hide and Seek

I play hide and seek with me.
I wonder wherever I can be?
I look at the chair.
No, I'm not there.
I look at the mat.
No, that's the cat.
I wonder wherever I can be?
I look in the mirror and I find me!
D. E.

Guinea Pig

When guinea pig looked in the glass one day,
He shouted with a wail,
'Oh, dearie me. Why didn't you say,
That I had lost my tail?'
He looked to the left, he looked to the right;
He looked just everywhere.
He crawled in a corner to be out of sight.
He really had a scare.
His mother called, 'My son – come out.'
He crept out like a snail.
She said, 'My boy, there is no doubt –
YOU NEVER HAD A TAIL.'
D. E.

Kinkajou

Living in the zoo,
Is a baby kinkajou.
Every time I peep,
He's always fast asleep.
What a nice surprise,
If he opened up his eyes.
And said, 'How do you do,
I'm a baby kinkajou.'
D. E.

Mr Nobody

I know a funny little man,
As quiet as a mouse,
Who does the mischief that is done
In everybody's house!
There's no one ever sees his face,
And yet we all agree
That every plate we break was cracked
By Mr Nobody.

The finger marks upon the door
By none of us are made;
We never leave the blinds unclosed
To let the curtains fade.
The ink we never spill, the boots
That lying round you see
Are not our boots; they all belong
To Mr Nobody.

Me

When I was one,
I was very small.
I was not very fat,
I was not very tall.
I had tiny feet
And tiny toes,
Tiny fingers
And a tiny nose!

A little bit bigger,
Each day I grew.
I looked at me
When I was two.
I could jump,
I could run,
I could talk,
It was fun!

I grew some more
And now I'm three.
I feel so big
When I look at me.
I have bigger feet
And bigger toes,
Bigger fingers
And a bigger nose!
D. E.

Losing Things

I'm very good at losing things,
Especially things in twos.
Like socks and gloves and mittens,
And even boots and shoes.
There's always one –
                that seems to stay.
And always one –
                that hides away!

D. E.

Keys

Keys are used to wind up clocks.
They undo things and fit in locks.
Keys are fat – or thin – or small.
Keys are short – or long – or tall.
But there is one that puzzles me –
It's in a cage – what can it be?

Children guess.
A monkey.

D. E.

Mouse

We have a little mouse,
Who lives in our house.
His front door is so small,
It's hardly there at all.

I have not really tried,
But I'd like to look inside,
To see if he has toys,
Just like girls and boys!

D. E.

Jack in the Box

What can I see?
    It's a key!
Where does it go?
    I don't know!
It fits in here,
    give a cheer.
Open the box –
    out Jack pops!
    D. E.

Sometimes

Sometimes I play inside –
    sometimes I play out.
Sometimes I am quiet –
    sometimes I can shout!
Sometimes I help Mum –
    sometimes I help Dad.
Sometimes I am good –
    sometimes I am bad!
    D. E.

My Son John

Diddle, diddle, dumpling, my son John,
Went to bed with his trousers on.
One shoe off, the other shoe on,
Diddle, diddle, dumpling, my son John.

The Crooked Man

There was a crooked man,
And he went a crooked mile.
He found a crooked sixpence,
Against a crooked stile.
He bought a crooked cat,
Who caught a crooked mouse.
And they all lived together,
In a crooked little house.

Piggy on the Railway

Piggy on the railway,
Picking up stones.
Along came an engine
And broke poor piggy's bones.
'Oh!' said piggy,
'That's not fair.'
'Oh!' said the engine-driver,
'I don't care!'

Make a mask!

Dr Foster

Dr Foster went to Gloucester,
In a shower of rain.
He stepped in a puddle,
Right up to his middle.
And never went there again.

Rain

See the raindrops – how they glisten
On the window pane.
You can hear them, if you listen
To the dripping of the rain.
'I can beat you,' said the big drop,
'To the window ledge.'
He went so fast, he could not stop,
And slipped right off the edge!
D. E.

Pictures

I see pictures in the bubbles,
  I blow in my bath.
I see pictures in the puddles,
  I walk in on my path.
It's not really pictures,
  that I think I see.
It's just my *reflection*,
  looking back at me.
D. E.

Splish, Splosh

Dripping, dropping,
Splishing, sploshing,
On the window pane.
Plipping, plopping,
Never stopping,
Listen to the rain.
D. E.

The Little Nut Tree

I had a little nut tree, nothing would it bear,
But a silver nutmeg and a golden pear.
The king of Spain's daughter came to visit me,
All on account of my little nut tree.

The North Wind

The north wind doth blow,
And we shall have snow,
And what will the robin do then?
Poor thing.
He'll sit in a barn,
To keep himself warm,
And hide his head under his wing.
Poor thing.

Three Little Kittens

Three little kittens
Lost their mittens,
And they began to cry,
'Oh, mother dear, we sadly fear
Our mittens we have lost!'
'What! lost your mittens,
You naughty kittens!
Then you shall have no pie.'
'Meow, meow, meow!'

The three little kittens,
Found their mittens,
And they began to cry,
'Oh, mother dear, see here, see here,
Our mittens we have found.'
'What! found your mittens,
You good little kittens,
Then you shall have some pie.'
'Purr, purr, purr.'

Three Little Rats

Three little rats with black felt hats,
Three little ducks with cricket bats,
Three little dogs with curling tails,
Three little cats with bright red pails,
Went out to play with two little pigs,
In satin vests and curly wigs.
But suddenly it chanced to rain,
And so they all went home again.

Pussy Cat, Pussy Cat

Pussy cat, pussy cat,
Where have you been?
I've been to London
To visit the queen.
Pussy cat, pussy cat,
What did you there?
I frightened a little mouse.
Under the chair.

It's Raining

It's raining, it's pouring,
The old man's snoring.
He went to bed,
And bumped his head,
And couldn't get up in the morning.

SAFETY RHYMES

Fireworks

Fireworks are pretty – but fireworks hop!
Fireworks sparkle – but fireworks pop!
Some go up – some go round;
Some go bang – with a very loud sound.
The bonfire's hot – so well back we stand,
Making sure we hold a grown-up's hand.
Fireworks are pretty – but fireworks hop!
Fireworks sparkle – but fireworks pop!
D. E.

In the Car

We're going for a ride in somebody's car,
  somebody's car, somebody's car.
We're going for a ride in somebody's car,
We'll sit in the back 'cause it's safer there.

The ones in the front need a safety belt,
  a safety belt, a safety belt.
The ones in the front need a safety belt.
Always remember to 'belt up' and take care!
D. E.

Colours

Think of two colours,
   What can they be?
Look all around you,
   What can you see?
Penguins, zebras, pandas,
   In the zoo.
Badgers in the wood,
   Are the same colour too.
Look for a crossing,
   To cross the road right.
The colours that we see
   Are . . .
Children guess.
D. E.

Look

Somewhere in the town,
There's a funny little man.
If he's red you *cannot* cross,
If he's green, you *can*!

Where is he?
Overlooking the pedestrian crossing.
D. E.

8
Fingers, Feet, and Fun!

All Kinds of Rhymes for Special Occasions

Making a Cake

Children stand in a circle round a pretend bowl.

What are we going to make?
I know – a birthday cake!
Put in sugar and stir it well.
    Pretend to put in and stir.
It's going to be good, I can tell.

This part can be said over and over again, putting in many different things – including nasties!

Magic, magic, make it bake.
> *Wave arms around.*

Look at our enormous cake.
> *Arms wide.*

Take a piece, taste it too.
> *Pretend to cut and taste.*

What's it like?
Ooo! Ooo! Ooo!

This can be a nice or a nasty sound, depending on ingredients!
D. E.

Twinkle, Twinkle

Twinkle, twinkle, little star,
> *Looking upwards.*

How I wonder what you are.
Up above the world so high,
> *Pointing upwards.*

Like a diamond in the sky.

When the blazing sun is gone,
When he nothing shines upon,
Then you show your little light,
Twinkle, twinkle, all the night.

Birthday Candles

How many candles on the birthday cake?
How many candles did they make?
I can see — all burning bright.
> *Use the child's age and hold up fingers.*

All blow together to put out a light.
> *Blow fingers and fold one finger down.*

How many candles on the birthday cake?
How many candles did they make?
I can see — all burning bright.
> *One less.*

All blow together to put out a light.
> *Blow fingers and fold another down.*

Continue until there are no 'candles' left, then:
All out now – let's have a slice.
> *Pretend to cut cake.*

This birthday cake tastes very nice!
> *Lick lips and pretend to eat.*

D. E.

I Am a Christmas Tree

I am a pretty Christmas tree,
    Stand straight.
Standing in a pot for all to see.
My branches are covered in tinsel bright,
    Spread arms to indicate branches.
Wound round and round – a little too tight.
    Wriggle slightly.
I've parcels hanging all about,
    Look down at pretend parcels.
If one's too heavy, I can't shout.
    Pretend one is heavy by lowering arm.
It's nice when they water my feet.
    Wriggle feet.
'Cause I really do feel the heat.
    Pretend to be hot.
And at night when everyone's gone to bed.
I shake myself from toe to head.
    Have a good shake.
D. E.

Christmas is Coming

Christmas is coming,
And the goose is getting fat.
Please put a penny in the old man's hat.
If you haven't got a penny,
A ha'penny will do.
If you haven't got a ha'penny –
God bless you!

Crackers

Five big crackers in a box;
Five fingers held up.
Let's pull one until it pops.
Pretend to hold one end in each hand. Pull and then shout 'pop!'.
Four big crackers, etc.
Continue rhyme until there are none left, then:
My box is empty, it's not full.
There's no more crackers left to pull.
D. E.

My Card

I sent a card to my friend,
   and he sent one to me.
My friend asked me,
   and I asked him:
Please can you come to tea?

I went to his house,
   and he came to mine.
We got in such a muddle,
   for tea there was no time.
D. E.

Hot Cross Buns

Hot cross buns, hot cross buns;
One a penny, two a penny,
Hot cross buns.

Hot cross buns, hot cross buns;
If you have no daughters,
Give them to your sons!

Index of First Lines

Baa-baa black sheep, 61
The big old clock, 43

Can you walk on tiptoe?, 39
Christmas is coming, 102
Come and watch me sewing, 19
A cow goes moo – its calf goes maa, 70

Diddle, diddle, dumpling, my son John, 87
Dr Foster went to Gloucester, 88
Dripping, dropping, 89

A family of fingers going for a walk, 14
Feet together, standing still, 33
The Finger Family thinks it's night, 79
The Finger Family want to play, 80
Fireworks are pretty – but fireworks hop!, 94
Five big crackers in a box, 102
Five fish fingers, 28
Five little fingers walked across my lap, 24
Five little frogs, 30
Five little Indians dancing round and round, 27
Five red round balloons, 26

Heads and shoulders, knees and toes, 52
Here we go round the mulberry bush, 62
Hickory, dickory, dock, 22
Hot cross buns, hot cross buns, 103
How many candles on the birthday cake?, 100

I am a baby fast asleep, 50
I am a pretty Christmas tree, 101

I can see a caterpillar, 17
If I could wish what I could be, 49
I had a little nut tree, 90
I hear thunder, I hear thunder, 72
I know a funny little man, 84
I looked in the mirror, 85
I'm a little teapot, 41
I'm inside an egg, with a shell all round, 47
I'm very good at losing things, 86
Incy Wincy Spider climbed up the spout, 16
I play hide and seek with me, 83
I see pictures in the bubbles, 90
I sent a card to my friend, 103
It's raining, it's pouring, 93
I went up one pair of stairs, 82

Jumping, jumping – jumping man, 34

Keys are used to wind up clocks, 86

Let's pretend to be a frog, 51
Little Arabella Miller, 21
Little Robin Redbreast, 38
Little Robin Redbreast sat upon a tree, 44
London Bridge is falling down, 60
Lots and lots of funny clowns, 53
Living in the zoo, 84

Marching, marching, marching two by two, 32
Miss Polly had a dolly, 48
Mr Conductor had a band, 56
My finger is a monkey, 15
My little house won't stand up straight, 15

The north wind doth blow, 90

Old John Muddlecombe lost his cap, 50
One finger and one finger, 25
One little mouse crept out one day, 16
One, two, buckle my shoe, 29
One, two, three, four, five, 30

Pat-a-cake, pat-a-cake, 70
Peter hammers with one hammer, 40
Piggy on the railway, 88
Polly put the kettle on, 55
Push your lips out, 71
Pussy cat, pussy cat, 93

Quietly, quietly, not a sound, 69

Riding in a train I go, 45
Ring a ring of roses, 64
Ring the bell, 42
Round and round the garden, 20
Running, running, on the spot, 35

See me curl up very small, 46
See the raindrops – how they glisten, 89
Sometimes I play inside, 87
Somewhere in the town, 96

There was a crooked man, 88
There was a little girl, 42
There was an old man called Michael Finnigin, 59
Think of two colours, 95
This little piggy went to market, 36
Three little kittens, 91
Three little rats with black felt hats, 92
Tiptoe softly like a mouse, 39
A tortoise has a house that goes everywhere with it, 39
Twinkle, twinkle, little star, 99
Two feet together, then lift up one, 32
Two little dicky-birds, 18

Up the tall white candlestick, 20
Up, up, up and up so high, 80

Washing in the washing machine, 41
We have a little mouse, 86
We're going for a ride in somebody's car, 95
What are we going to make?, 98
What can I see?, 87
What do you suppose?, 21
The wheels on the bus go round and round, 58
When guinea pig looked in the glass one day, 83
When I was one, 84
When we wake up, we jump out of bed, 54
Wriggle your fingers and wriggle your toes, 38